30 MINUTES TO PEAK THINKING

How to Change Your Life Through Your Thoughts

BENJAMIN T. MUELLER

Copyright © Benjamin T. Mueller

All Rights Reserved

ISBN: 979-8-6475-9419-8

Cover photo by photographer Jacqueline Fouche, from
freeimages.com

This book provides content related to physical and/or mental health issues. As such, use of this book implies your acceptance of this disclaimer. This book details the author's personal experiences with and opinions about health and fitness. The author is not a healthcare provider. The author and publisher are providing this book and its contents on an "as is" basis and make no representations or warranties of any kind with respect to this book or its contents. The author and publisher disclaim all such representations and warranties, including for example warranties of merchantability and healthcare for a particular purpose. In addition, the author and publisher do not represent or warrant that the information accessible via this book is accurate, complete or current.

The author, publisher, and contributors will not be liable for damages arising out of or in connection with the use of this book. This is a comprehensive limitation of liability that applies to all damages of any kind, including (without limitation) compensatory; direct, indirect or consequential damages; loss of data, income or profit; loss of or damage to property and claims of third parties.

You understand that this book is not intended as a substitute for consultation with a licensed healthcare practitioner, such as your physician. Before you begin any healthcare program, exercise program, or change your lifestyle in any way, you should consult your physician or another licensed healthcare practitioner to ensure you are in good health and that the examples contained in this book will not harm you. The authors and publisher advise readers to take full responsibility for their safety and know their limits.

I would like to thank everyone who has had a positive impact on my life. This includes past teachers, family, friends, students, and coworkers. Your inspiration has been a huge part of my life.

Special thanks to Leigh Kossman, who wrote the foreword to this book, and to my editor, Kathryn Galán. Your hard work means the world to me.

I would also like to give a shout out and thanks to Joe Patrick for pointing me in the right direction regarding mental health and the positive power of thought.

CONTENTS

"Change your thoughts, change your life."

—Dr. Wayne W. Dyer

Foreword

WHEN OUR OLDEST DAUGHTER started high school in 2008, I met Ben Mueller. He was her teacher for health class. Wellness is something we have always valued in our family, and often our daughter would relate what she'd learned in Ben's class to our practices at home.

When my husband and I went to our first teacher's conference with Ben, it was apparent that we were kindred souls. A few years later, I became a substitute teacher and got to know Ben even better. Our conversations about health and wellness were never at a loss! We like to compare notes, affirm each other, and share resources.

Reading Ben's second book, *The Operating Manual for Great Health,* was a pleasure! It's concise, easy to read, and offers a very comprehensive, solid overview. In addition, Ben's suggestions for improving all aspects of one's health aren't overwhelming and are very doable ways to get started at being (more) healthy. This new book offers the reader more of the same!

"Five Essentials to Health" are recommended in Ben's second book, referenced above. While I subscribe to all of them, I am particularly passionate about the fifth he presents, which is, "Maximized Mind/Mindset: Having a positive mindset, outlook, and thought process." Though having recently been called to life coaching, my first formal education endeavor was pursuing a graduate certification in positive psychology (University of Missouri). Following that, I received formal training and certification from the JRNI Coaching Intensive and ICF (International Coach Federation).

It's amazing how so much of what goes on in our lives is directly and specifically related to what swirls around in our heads, the things we tell ourselves, and the resultant actions! Never before has mindset been so scientifically studied, documented, and shown to influence outcome. In *60 Minutes to Peak Mental Health*, Ben Mueller captures so many of the tenets and practices of positive psychology and living a healthy life, in ways beyond the physical self.

Relaxation exercises (including meditation and guided imagery), conquering fear, visualization, affirmations, goal-setting, values, healthy relationships, self-awareness, empathetic listening, and a kind approach are just a handful of the key topics that Ben covers so well. His easy style of writing, checklists, "Did You Know?" facts, stats, and quotes make for an enjoyable, educational read!

Ben, your book will be a welcomed addition to your readers' libraries! I'm grateful and honored that you asked me to write your foreword. I look forward to our continued conversations about positivity, health, and wellness.

God Bless You and Cheers, my friend!

Leigh-Leigh Kossman
Get Your Shit Together Coaching
Facebook: Get Your Shit Together Coaching
www.coachinggyst.com

"Words are very powerful. They have the ability to create a moment and the strength to destroy the moment."

—Susan Gale

About This Book

30 MINUTES IS THE AVERAGE amount of time it will take a person to read this entire short book. Depending upon your reading speed, it may take you a little less or a little more.

What can you accomplish in thirty minutes? What if I told you, after reading this book, you will be equipped with the power to change your life?

"Change your thoughts, change your life." This quote by the great Dr. Wayne Dyer is so true! Our thinking literally controls our habits, actions, goals, passions, motivation, current emotions, and success.

One of the most fascinating things to me is the fact that the placebo effect works a great deal of the time. Simply *believing* you have some advantage actually *gives* you an advantage. That belief stems from our thoughts!

The difference between achievers and non-achievers can simply be the way that they think. Can we actually train the way we think? Can we actually get ourselves to think differently? The answer is, *YES!*

Just like anything worth doing, it does take practice and effort to shift our thinking. It also takes a great deal of reflection and looking back at our thoughts and decisions.

We have all sat through motivational speeches before. Usually, we feel some sort of empowerment after the talk. But research has shown that very few people actually take action based on those speeches, and most people return back to their regular habits and old ways of thinking very quickly. The vast majority of people leave those so-called motivational speeches full of energy and excitement, only to change very little later on.

In this book, you will learn what causes your thoughts. We look at why we oftentimes think negatively. You will learn ways of improving your thoughts and habits, plus find specific exercises that will turn you into a positive thinker.

With that, I leave you to enjoy this book. Happy thinking! May your thoughts guide you in the right direction.

The Power of Positive Thinking

WHEN YOU WAKE UP, are you excited for the challenges that lie ahead? The truth is most people wake up and immediately begin to think negative thoughts. That is, many people mentally beat themselves up before they even start their day. It is important we do not do this to ourselves!

Your actions are always a reflection of your thoughts. If you think more positive thoughts, you will get better results. As I begin this book, I wish help to you analyze the way we think and look at the impact thoughts can have on your health.

Most of the mental toxins we allow to enter our mind are thoughts related to fear, failure, anger, jealousy, greed, sadness, and anxiety. If we allow these mental toxins to fill our mind, then we will never get the most out of our life. These toxins not only cause us to think negatively, but they also prevent us from reaching our peak potential. It is important for us to remember that thoughts affect our physical health as well as our mental health. (Later on, we will discuss how stress affects your physical body in a negative way, too.)

One way to get rid of toxic thoughts is simply to fill your mind with nurturing thoughts. I like to think of these nurturing thoughts as vegetables for your mind. They help your mind detoxify, and they nourish it with positive energy. We simply function better when we are in a state of compassion and bliss.

The following are thoughts and actions that lead to a better overall health:

➢ Being happy for others
➢ Putting yourself in others' shoes, and having compassion
➢ Volunteering to help those in need
➢ Being grateful for what you do have
➢ Greeting change with excitement
➢ Being optimistic about your chances of success
➢ Taking on a growth mindset toward new challenges

The following is a set of quotes that should help put your mindset in the right spot:

* ✳ "Make forgiveness your highest function; that means forgive others and yourself."
* ✳ "Greet change with openness and expect that change will happen."
* ✳ "Take time to ponder and meditate. Enjoying the present moment is key."
* ✳ "Let your dreams be your guide, not your fears."
* ✳ "True failure is the act of giving up."

###

Did you know?

The placebo effect has been shown to work in multiple studies. The simple belief that a person has an advantage is oftentimes enough to actually help them improve.

Spirituality

RELIGION AND SPIRITUALITY are perhaps the most important topics we learn about and engage in. Even if you do not believe in a particular religion, there is connectedness between nature, people, our planet, and beyond.

In this book, I will not slant my views toward any one particular religion, but I will focus on the positives that all of the major religions share. After studying all of the major religions, they all seem to have the following in common:

* **Compassion**: To make the world a better place, we must have compassion for one another. We must be willing to put ourselves in others' shoes and understand that everyone is going through their own personal struggles.

* **Courage**: It is essential we have the courage to conquer our fears, the courage to strive to make ourselves better individuals, and the courage to stand up for what we believe in. People have an endless amount of courage. This should allow us to follow our hearts.

* **Empowerment**: Anyone can point out the problems of the world, but very few people are empowered to create change. We all have an unlimited amount of empowerment that will not only allow us to not succumb to the negative influences of the world, but will also support us in creating positive energy and change.

* **Love:** Gandhi, Jesus, and many other wise teachers believed that love was a powerful force. We have an infinite amount of love! That love should not only be directed at our immediate families. It should extend to everyone on the planet. Love is the force that binds us together and keeps everyone safe.

###

Controlling Stress

DO YOU FIND yourself stressed out all the time? Are you easily angered? Does life feel difficult most of the time? Do you feel you are unable to control your stress? If you answered yes to any of these questions, your stress may be taking a toll on your health.

Imagine you are enjoying a picnic on a nice sunny day. You are with your friends, enjoying fun games and good food. Then, out of nowhere comes this large, angry bear. The bear looks furious, and immediately you feel threatened. You now have a choice to either run away from the bear or fight the bear.

Imagine how the threat of this bear will change the physiology of your body. Your heart rate will go up, breathing will become faster, muscles will tense, blood pressure increases, blood sugar increases, sweating begins, your senses will sharpen, and your brain will switch into survival mode. These changes will help you either fight or run away from the bear. On the other hand, any body system not needed to run away or fight will turn off. This includes your digestive, reproductive, and immune systems.

In the bear example, it is beneficial for your body to go through the stress response. After all, the stress response will put you in the best position to run or fight the bear. For the most part, the stress response is only useful when our life is in immediate danger.

The problem is humans let themselves get in the stress response for things that are not life-threatening. Our adrenal glands store adrenaline for emergency response to a threatening situation. We do not want to tap into this adrenaline too often, however, or it can damage our body's ability to heal.

When it comes to your health, stress is not your friend. Because your immune system is shut off during the stress response, constant stress increases your risk of getting sick.

The following is a list of some of the short-term effects stress has on the body:

✓ Muscles tense
✓ Pupils dilate
✓ Sense of hearing improves

- ✓ Logical thinking is impaired, and reptile brain turns on
- ✓ Heart rate and breathing increase
- ✓ Blood pressure rises
- ✓ Blood sugar rises
- ✓ Immune system is impaired
- ✓ Digestive system is impaired
- ✓ Reproductive system is impaired

The short-term effects of stress are your body's response to get out of danger. The problem becomes when we are constantly under stress, because our body's systems eventually become overloaded.

The following are some of the long-term effects of chronic stress:

- ✓ Higher risk of heart diseases (due to wear and tear on your heart and blood)
- ✓ Higher risk of viral and bacterial infections (due to immune system being suppressed)
- ✓ Back aches and headaches (due to muscle tension)
- ✓ Digestive and reproductive system problems (due to impairment of these systems)
- ✓ Higher risk of depression
- ✓ Anger levels may get higher

Because of the dangerous short- and long-term effects of stress, it is important we manage our stress. Stress cannot be eliminated from our lives, but it can greatly be reduced by coming up with a good stress management action plan.

This action plan will look different for everyone. The following are some tips on managing stress.

> ➤ Make sure to get regular physical activity. The activity can be anything you want, but make sure to exercise for at least thirty minutes daily.

> ➤ Make sure to get enough sleep. Sleep is critical to reducing stress! If you miss out on sleep, you will be under more stress in the short and long term.

> ➤ Learn relaxation exercises that can help your body get out of the stress response. Possible relaxation exercises are yoga, meditation, deep breathing, and guided imagery.

> ➤ Take time to do things you enjoy. As simple as this sounds, it is amazing how many people do not do this.

> ➤ For some, reading, art, or puzzles is a great way to manage stress.

- ➢ Avoid dangerous activities that many people use to deal with stress, such as alcohol, drugs, or violent behavior.
- ➢ Explore a variety of different stress-management techniques. You should soon learn what works for you.

Did you know?

Stress can come from both external and internal sources. It can be argued most of the stress we experience today comes from our own thoughts. Because of this, you can reduce your stress by changing the way you think and by framing your thoughts in a different way.

Two great questions to ask yourself when you feel stress coming on are:

- ❖ Is my life in danger?
- ❖ Will the stress response help the situation?

If the answer is no to both, then tell yourself that stressing out is not worth it.

Relaxation Exercises

CHANGING THE WAY you think and following a healthy lifestyle can together greatly reduce the amount of stress in your daily life. Adequate sleep, nutrition, and exercise are three key strategies to combat stress. In addition to these, I would like to introduce another lifestyle behavior that can greatly reduce your overall stress and improve your health: relaxation exercises.

There are several relaxation exercises you can experiment with to see which ones work best for you. Like anything else, it takes regular practice with them to get the maximum benefits.

Each of these relaxation exercises is designed to shift your body out of the stress response. When you free your body from constant stress response, your body will be in the best position to heal itself.

The relaxation exercises below are very simple and can be done by anyone. You will get the best results and greatest benefit from these exercises when you do them regularly. There are others not mentioned in this book, but these are the ones I have had the greatest success with.

Meditation:

- Find a comfortable place free of distractions.
- Sit down, and keep your posture balanced. Do not slouch!
- Place your hands wherever you want.
- Decide on a word or phrase to repeat.
- Close your eyes, and continue to repeat the word or phrase in your mind.
- Your only intention is to get back to that word. If your mind drifts away, just focus on repeating the word or phrase.
- Perform this for about ten to twenty minutes.
- Come out of your meditation slowly!

Guided Imagery:

- Look up a guided-imagery video.
- You can sit or lie down on your back.
- Close your eyes and listen to video.
- Come out of the guided imagery exercise slowly.

Deep breathing:

- Take five deep breaths in and out.
- Ask yourself: *Is my life in danger?*
- Ask yourself: *Is being in the stress response helpful?*
- Your answers should always be *no* to both questions, unless you really are in danger.
- Then take five deep breaths again.

Did you know?

Studies show that meditation activates the deep brain waves that otherwise are activated only during deep sleep. These are the brain waves that promote rest and recovery.

"*Everything you want is on the other side of fear.*"

—Jack Canfield

Conquering Fear

FEAR IS THE EMOTION that comes from the thought, *If I do this, then something bad will happen.* Fear is only useful in instances when it prevents us from doing something that may damage us. For example, fear is what prevents you from crossing the street when a car is coming. Fear is what prevents you from gambling away all your money at a casino. Fear is completely natural and useful in many instances.

The problem arises when we let fear stop us from growing as an individual. When you are afraid to take smart risks, you limit your capabilities as an individual. Because of this, we need be aware of the fears we have and be willing to conquer them.

For example, many people fear what others will think of them. This is common and something we do not want or need to fear. If we spend our whole life worrying about what others think of us, we will not accomplish much. Never let your wellness or personal growth suffer because of a fear of what others may think of you.

The following are some tips on conquering your fears:

> Look up the statistics on your fear. For example, if you get anxious at the idea of flying in an airplane, you could learn about how you have a better chance of being in a car accident than a plane accident.
> Realize that experience is key to getting over your fear. For example, the best way to conquer a fear of public speaking, if that makes you nervous, is finding ways to practice and to do it multiple times with slowly growing audiences.
> Talk about your fear with someone who does the thing you're afraid of, and come up with strategies to overcome it.
> Realize single no fear is common among all people. There are always others who do not share your fear, so what can you learn from them?
> Admit your fear, and realize that it can be unlearned.

###

Did you know?

It has been said that more people fear public speaking than death. Once you free yourself of the fear of what others think, you become free as an individual to express yourself in many wonderful ways.

26

"He who angers you, controls you."

—Author unknown

Anger Management

MANAGING YOUR ANGER is critical for gaining control of your mental health. Anger comes from the thought, *This should not be happening right now*. Think about it! Every time you have gotten angry in the past, this thought always raged through your mind.

Like fear and stress, anger is given to us for survival reasons. About the only time anger does us any good is in situations where something or someone is attacking us. Then, anger causes our adrenaline to rise and flood our system, putting our bodies in the best position to fight our attacker.

When we let anger flood our mind, it really affects our health and thinking. We do not think well when we are in a state of anger. There is a lot of truth to the saying, "Anger makes us stupid." For our health and relationships, it is essential we learn to manage our anger.

The following are tips for managing anger:

- ✓ Take stress management seriously, and be vigilant about noticing, calming, and improving your stress levels.
- ✓ Perform relaxation exercises such as meditation and yoga on a regular basis.
- ✓ Keep up with an exercise routine. Exercise enhances our mood!
- ✓ Reflect on why you get angry, and keep a journal.
- ✓ Make sure to get enough sleep, as sleep deprivation leads us to getting angry quickly.
- ✓ Always try to respond in an assertive, kind, and compassionate manner.

Did you know?

One of the first signs of sleep deprivation is being easily angered.

"If you are searching for that one person who will change your life, take a look in the mirror."

—Author unknown

Visualization

VISUALIZING YOURSELF reaching your goals is an important part of the process of successful attaining what you set out to do. Many successful athletes, for example, use visualization as a tool to help them reach peak performance.

Billy Mills, who won the 10,000 metres gold medal at the 1968 Tokyo Olympics, visualized himself winning the race dozens of times every day for years before the race. Once the race day came, he pulled off one of the greatest upsets in Olympic history.

I suggest creating a vision board for yourself and updating it regularly. Vision boards can be created on your smart phone, computer, or on paper. Put together pictures and images that represent you reaching your goals and confirming your affirmations. Display it somewhere where you can see it regularly.

Visualization helps your mind perceive success before it happens. As Billy Mills says, "The subconscious mind does not know the difference between reality and imagination."

###

Did you know?

Vision boards allow you to use imagery as a way to ignite your passion, goals, and affirmations. Making an electronic vision board is great, because you can update it easily with your new goals.

"If you do what you've always done, you'll get what you've always gotten."

—Tony Robbins

Affirmations

SETTING AFFIRMATIONS is a great way to change behavior. An affirmation is a positive statement, usually written in "I am" form. Writing your affirmation down on paper, posting it in as many places as possible, and repeating it to yourself regularly are keys to the process.

You want to choose and focus affirmations for areas of your life that you tend to think about negatively, as these less-than-positive thoughts will likely cause you not to perform well or achieve your goals. For example, if you feel you do not make good dietary choices, you could set an affirmation toward healthier eating.

Your affirmation may be something along the lines of, "I eat healthy foods every day." By writing this down and repeating it to yourself, you should notice, after some time, your dietary choices improve and become better. For example, you may choose a piece of fruit instead of a candy bar as a snack. Over time, you should notice yourself making better choices around your eating and nutrition.

When creating affirmations, it is important to state them in the present tense. Affirmations are not goals! They need to be written in the form that shows you presently have that skill or trait. Affirmations work at realigning thoughts in your mind so that, eventually, you repeat more positive thoughts.

It will take time and practice to successfully change your thoughts. You will find yourself swaying off of your affirmation every now and then. When this happens, it is important to continue to repeat the affirmation in your head and not give up. Continue to repeat it, and you will notice that positive changes will happen.

Did you know?

An effective affirmation works to "rewire" your subconscious mind to spit out more positive thoughts in your conscious mind. It will take time to "rewire" your subconscious mind.

"When you let your values guide your decisions, decision making becomes easier."

—Dr. Michael Olpin

"Finally, I am coming to the conclusion that my highest ambition is to be what I already am. That I will never fulfill my obligation to surpass myself, unless I first accept myself, and if I accept myself fully in the right way, I will already have surpassed myself."

—Thomas Merton

Values

IF YOU ARE an adult, think about what you enjoyed doing as a child, and ask yourself whether you are still doing those things today. Now, I know what you are thinking. You're thinking you are grown up, likely have a job and family, so you do not have time to enjoy the same activities. Maybe you are thinking that playing is for kids. Perhaps you are thinking you have outgrown that lifestyle.

"We don't stop playing because we grow old; we grow old because we stop playing."

I believe there is a lot of truth to this quote by George Bernard Shaw. For people to achieve great mental health, they need to continue to explore their passions, learn more, and try new things. It is only when we stop exploring and growing that we truly stagnate in life.

One of the core principles to achieving excellent mental health is to live a life according to your values. This is key to achieving a life of happiness and success. As simple as this is, it is amazing how most people do not live a life according to their values. This is the source of a lot of problems in people's lives today with regards to their mental health.

We all make decisions every day. Some are little decisions, such as what are we going to eat for lunch, and others are major decisions, such as what career field to go into. Making decisions can be very stressful; often, we weigh out the pros and cons of each decision. When you let your values guide your decisions, making decisions becomes easier.

The first step is discovering what your values truly are. This requires you have an honest conversation with yourself and think about what you truly stand for as a person. An easy way to do this is to imagine you are at your own funeral at some point in the future. What would you want your friends, family, co-workers, and everyone who knew you to say about you? What would you want to be remembered for?

Those traits are what you should strive for in your life and the values that should guide your decisions. Ultimately, if we let our values guide our decisions, we will be happier and achieve the life we want to live.

###

Did you know?

Despite having the highest standard of living, Americans report having more mental health problems than other less-developed countries.

Self-Awareness

WE ALL NEED to have an honest conversation with ourselves about our biases and the weaknesses in our interpersonal interactions with others. Everyone has biases, and if we fail to recognize our own, they can lead us down the wrong path. Once we know our biases and admit we have them, however, we will be more in control of ourselves and can prevent them from driving or interfering with our interactions with others.

Typically, we judge others based on our first impressions of them and then justify that judgment based on what happens after that. For example, if we judge someone to be a bad person, after that, we tend to see more of the bad in them than the good.

This can skew our view of others and wreck our chances at developing a strong relationship with that person.

###

Did you know?

Social intuition is the degree to which you can read the feelings of others in various social situations. People with great social intuition know the best way to respond to others in a situation.

Empathetic Listening

OFTEN, PEOPLE JUST want someone to talk to about their problems. If you find yourself in a situation where someone is communicating their distress to you, you can practice empathetic listening.

Empathetic listening is a technique we can use to show care, compassion, and empathy for someone who is communicating with us. The following are the different components of empathetic listening:

* Give the speaker good eye contact while they are talking.

* Do not multi-task! Doing so will lead them to believe their concern is not important to you.

* Give them nonverbal cues of understanding, such as a head nod, to show them you are listening.

* Do not interrupt them! Let them talk, and wait for your turn to speak.

* When they are done speaking, ask clarifying questions or summarize what they told you. For example, "So my understanding is…" This gives them the impression you care.

* Do not feel you must immediately offer advice. It is okay to admit you are not sure of the best way to resolve their concerns or situation.

* Do tell them you feel bad for them and that they are on your mind.

When you use this technique, others will be appreciative of your willingness to help them. Many times, they just want someone to talk to, and oftentimes, the person will come up with a solution on their own. They may come to you more often and view you as someone they can trust.

Of course, not everyone likes to talk about their problems. We must be respectful of that, too.

###

Did you know?

Many times, people just want someone to communicate their problems to or they need to share their struggles with someone. Oftentimes, just listening to them empathetically will help them out.

Assertive Approach

HAVING AN ASSERTIVE approach when interacting with others is key. Being assertive allows you to communicate with others in an appropriate way when they have crossed into your "do not enter" territory. Being assertive is about not coming across as overly aggressive but, at the same time, not being passive.

Being assertive is the best way to deal with confrontations with others and get the best results while not coming across as an angry lunatic. The following are some examples of ways to take a more assertive approach to people and situations:

➢ Tell others when you are upset and why something bothers you.
➢ Admit when you are wrong, and apologize to others.

> ➤ Be willing to forgive others when they admit they were wrong.
> ➤ Be firm with your decisions, and tell others why you made them.
> ➤ Compliment others on their achievements and do not get jealous.
> ➤ Do not yell or shout; instead, speak in a confident tone of voice.
> ➤ Talk over phone or in person when communicating something important.
> ➤ Always make decisions with your values in mind.

You will find that being assertive will make you a happier, more confident individual. Fewer people will try to walk over you. Best of all, you will be able to communicate your feelings effectively to others.

Did you know?

Being assertive will increase your chances of achieving inner peace. People who are too passive will not attain true inner peace, because their feelings get bottled up inside.

A Kind Approach

A FAMOUS QUOTE by Maya Angelou states, "People will forget what you said, people will forget what you did, but people will not forget how you made them feel."

We should always be as kind as possible to everyone! As the great Tom Shadyak says, "Humans function better in a state of kindness and empathy for others."

Because of this, we should make it our fundamental goal always to be kind and considerate of others.

###

Did you know?

Research has shown that people who volunteer to help others tend to live longer and are generally happier people. Continue to seek out ways to bring others up and make other people feel good about themselves.

Summary

> ➤ Positive thinking requires us to control our stress.

> ➤ You have the power to perceive any task or situation as either an exciting opportunity or a stressor.

> ➤ Relaxation exercises such as meditation and guided imagery can help reduce our long-term stress and anxiety.

> ➤ Fear and anger are two emotions that can be controlled by changing the way we think.

> ➤ Visualization and affirmations are effective tools we can use to change our subconscious mind and habits.

> ➤ To reach a high level of mental health, we must live a life according to our values.

> ➢ Being self-aware of our biases and faults is an important step toward connecting with others and reaching your peak mental health.

> ➢ It is important we take an assertive approach and respect ourselves when dealing with confrontations.

I hope you enjoyed this book and found something to inspire your peak mental health or try as new attitudes or approaches. Please do not hesitate to contact me at Ben.Mueller7@aol.com with any questions or requests for follow-up information.

With that, I wish you years of happy health. May all your goals and dreams come true.

Recommended Resources.

THE FOLLOWING FILMS and books taught and inspired me to formulate a successful strategy for living and feeling healthful and well. I encourage you to check them out!

Films:

> *Stress: Portrait of a Killer*
>
> *I AM*

Books:

> *Unwind* by Dr. Michael Olpin and Sam Bracken
>
> *Life's Operating Manual* by Tom Shadyak

What Now

BEN IS AVAILABLE to do speaking engagements. Invite him to talk to your group about applying the principles mentioned in this book.

Please contact Ben through email at Ben.Mueller7@aol.com. He can do presentations that vary from thirty minutes to an hour or two- and four-hour workshops. Each presentation can be tailored to meet your group's needs and interests.

About Ben

BEN MUELLER IS a wellness educator, endurance athlete, speaker, and activist. He has taught high school and junior college health and mathematics for over fifteen years.

Since he completed his first road race at the age of ten, Ben has not looked back. He is an avid runner and triathlete who has competed in over 500 road races, track races, and triathlons throughout the United States.

He qualified and competed in the United States national triathlon championships three times. He is also a Badger State Games (Wisconsin Olympics) gold medalist for multiple years in both the open and Masters categories.

Ben was born in Sheboygan, Wisconsin and went to college at UW-Whitewater. He earned his bachelor's degree in mathematics education and a master's degree in educational leadership at Concordia-Chicago. Currently, he is a doctoral student in education at Concordia-Chicago, doing his PhD research on exercise and its effects on coping with math anxiety.

When Ben is not training, he can be found refereeing soccer, rooting on the Wisconsin sports teams, or relaxing in a coffee shop.

Contact Ben here: Ben.mueller7@aol.com

Or find him here: BenjaminTMueller.webs.com

Also by Ben Mueller

Attain Peak Running Through Cross-Training

Attain Peak Referee Fitness

The Operating Manual for Great Health

www.ingramcontent.com/pod-product-compliance
Lightning Source LLC
Chambersburg PA
CBHW051415250726
48655CB00003B/1070